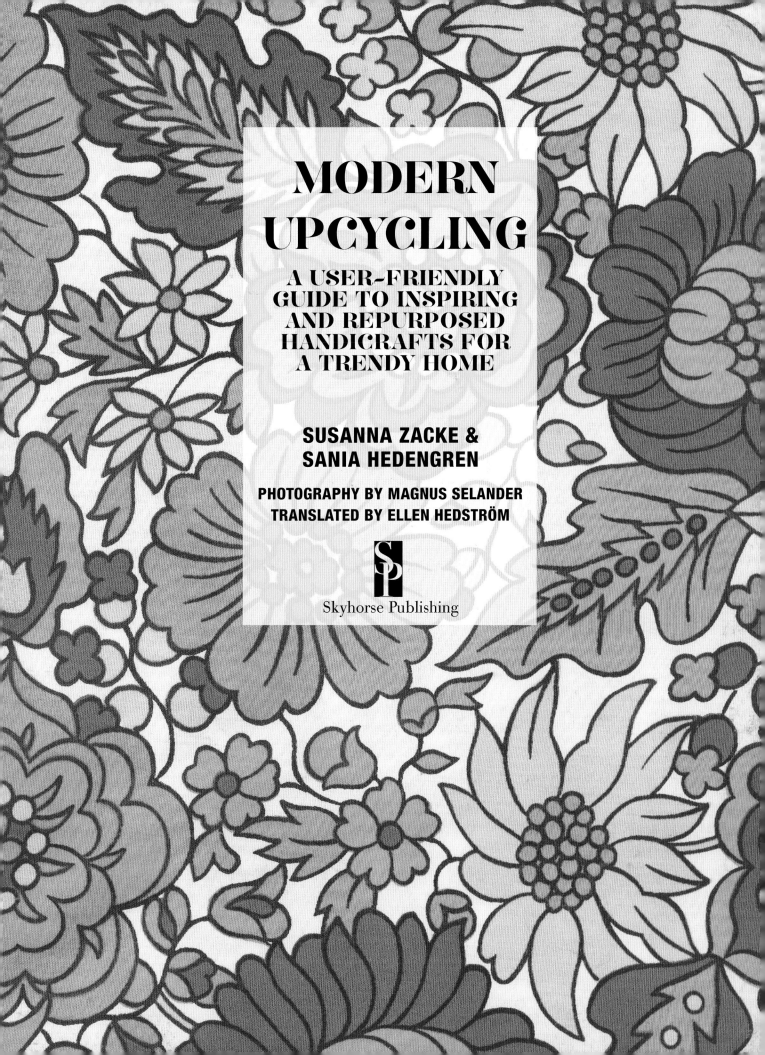

MODERN UPCYCLING

A USER-FRIENDLY GUIDE TO INSPIRING AND REPURPOSED HANDICRAFTS FOR A TRENDY HOME

SUSANNA ZACKE & SANIA HEDENGREN

PHOTOGRAPHY BY MAGNUS SELANDER
TRANSLATED BY ELLEN HEDSTRÖM

Skyhorse Publishing

CONTENTS

HANDICRAFTS
—homemade and personal!

The term "handicrafts" can sound both pretentious and a bit old-fashioned, but we think it represents something really wonderful, something that's been made by hand—a craftsmanship that needs to be preserved. Through this book, we want to inspire you to create your own crafts. We consider handicrafts to be something that you make with your own two hands, either for your own enjoyment or as a gift for loved ones.

Materials for handicrafts can vary. We have chosen to work with five specific types, all featured in their own chapter: fabric, wood, yarn, paper, and, last but not least, concrete. We have created items based on our own interests and put together layouts and interior designs that we hope will awaken the creativity within you.

We cast Easter eggs from concrete, crochet necklaces and bunting with yarn, and in the chapter on fabrics, our old vintage fabrics are featured as both a pouf and a lampshade. The garden bench where we grow things was made from an old mullioned window, and the towels in our bathroom are hung on a ladder made from branches. Old wallpaper can be used to cover bricks, cans, or vases. We'll also show you what you can do with a few pages from a secondhand book or an old rug.

We really hope you will enjoy modern, upcycled handicrafts!

Susanna & Sania

PS
We want to take the opportunity to thank ALL our readers, those of you who buy, read, or borrow our books. You let yourself be inspired by our ideas, you follow our blog, and you like what we do, and for that we want to give you a big THANK YOU!

FABRIC

We almost exclusively use vintage fabric when we work. Old comforters from the seventies are like gold to us, and we create new pillows, dresses, and curtains from them, or dress a lampshade in strips torn from a sheet. We love when the edges fray and it looks a bit worn. Kitchen towels and prettily embroidered tablecloths can also be put to good use. An antique sewing machine and old wooden spools are charming details that we leave out on display.

VINTAGE CUSHIONS

These cushions are made from duvet covers from the seventies, and to our thinking, this is as good as it gets. In the photograph on the previous page you can see many other lovely things made from fabric, such as a dress, a seat, and several pillows. There is also a patchwork quilt made by someone else. A simple way to make a cushion cover is to sew it as you would a pillowcase, which means you need neither a zipper nor any buttons.

- Measure the pillow. Here we are using a pillow that measures 23½" (60 cm) in length and 20" (50 cm) in width.
- Cut the material so it measures 57" (145 cm) long and 20" (50 cm) wide, adding another ½" (1.5 cm) seam allowance all around.
- Hem the short ends.
- Fold the material in half, right sides together, but leave 10" (25 cm), which is then folded back. This piece will then be facing right side up.
- Pin the long ends together.
- Sew the long ends together.
- Look at a regular pillowcase to see how it's made.

PHOTO TO THE RIGHT: *The armchair was a bargain we found online. We wrapped the armrests in fabric strips.*

WRAP

The living room is decorated with gorgeous natural fabrics in rich patterns and colors. Our goal was to draw attention to the materials used—wood, flax, and burlap—and create a visually appealing color scheme. A fun detail that was easy to make is the armrest on the chair, which we wrapped in strips of fabric. The chair was a great bargain online, and it looks just at home in the room. The green plant, a cluster of flowers, and a few splashes of color just enhance the overall feel.

- Tear a piece of cotton material into 1" (2 cm) wide strips.
- Attach one of the ends to the armrest with a bit of glue.
- Wrap the strips as far down the armrest as you want and secure the end with some glue.

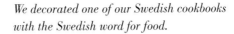

A COVERED COOKBOOK

Upcycle a cookbook by dressing it in fabric. It looks like art when left lying
around and also makes a unique gift.

- Cut the fabric to size, making sure you have an additional inch on each
  side. This allows you to fold the material around the edges of the cover.
- Print out large block letters on printer paper.
- Cut out the letters to make templates, place them on the back of another
  sheet of fabric, and trace them. Make sure the letters are placed according
  to their mirror image—facing the other direction.
- Cut out the fabric letters.
- Pin them to the fabric.
- Sew them onto the fabric using a zigzag seam.
- Use glue or Scotch tape to attach the fabric to the cover. Fold in the edges
  and attach these as well.

SLEEP TIGHT

A cozy place to rest your head. This bed, made with a mixture of old sheets, is
guaranteed to give you a peaceful night's rest and keep the bedbugs from
biting. We used a rose-patterned sheet and a neutral-colored duvet. The
pillowcase is decorated with embroidery we made on a sewing machine, and
the nightstand was created by turning a basket upside down.

Sew the pillowcase yourself and embroider it with a sewing machine. Many
modern machines have decorative stitching. We made pillowcases from a natural
linen fabric and decorated them with a pretty border in a contrasting color.

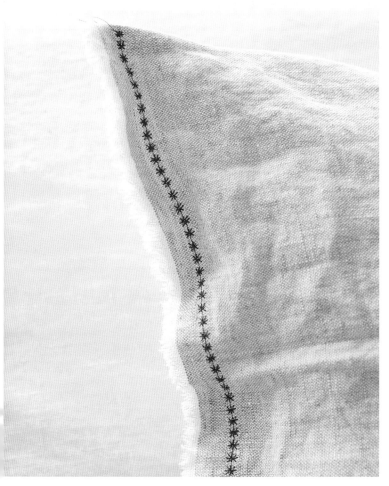

OLD AND NEW CUSHIONS

Ensure that your cushions catch your guests' eye by making new covers or by decorating your old ones with quaint vintage fabrics.

High-quality kitchen towels made from linen, embroidered textiles, and crocheted tablecloths are beautiful examples of handicrafts that should be cherished and displayed. Buy them in thrift stores, at yard sales, or at auctions and create something upcycled and personal. If you consider the number of hours spent making these pieces, the few dollars you have to spend really is a bargain.

We made a whole new cushion cover using two kitchen towels, and our two white cushions were both adorned with pieces of a tablecloth. One was crocheted and one was embroidered.

- Iron all the fabric, as this makes it easier to work with.
- Place the two towels with their right sides together and pin them.
- Sew three of the sides together using a machine, leaving roughly a ½" (1.5 cm) seam allowance.
- Turn it right-side out and place a cushion inside to make sure it fits.
- Place small pieces of cloth on each of the cushion covers and secure with pins.
- Sew them on.
- Place the cushions inside the covers.
- Sew the last end together or sew Velcro at the opening.

This metal stool was given a facelift with a new seat cover.

CHANGING WITH FABRIC

Dress a stool with fabric, sew fabric covers for your potted plants, and make some placemats out of burlap.

The spring sun shines in on this quaint dining area. Worn-out furniture can be spruced up with some nice fabric. A decorative ladder can be leaned against a wall and used as a storage solution for things like throw blankets, towels, or clothes.

STOOL COVER

- Measure the stool, add ½" (1.5 cm) seam allowance and cut the fabric: one round piece to cover the top of the seat and a rectangular strip of your desired width for the side.
- Sew the pieces together, right sides facing each other, and hem the bottom.
- Pull the cover over the stool and voilà, it's done!

FABRIC POTS

Sewing pot covers is easy. Why not make summer and winter pot covers and swap them out according to the season?

The standard, boring pots get a new spark of life with our springtime pot covers in white and pink. The cover is sewn in a tube shape that is simply pulled over the pot. Measure the pot, add a ½" (1.5 cm) seam allowance, and cut the fabric. Sew into a tube shape and hem the edges.

EASY PEASY

A black box with a pretty ribbon and blooming ranunculus planted inside . . . simple yet attractive.

RE-COVER

This old bench was transformed with a new cover that has a springtime pattern.

Measure and cut the fabric. Fold in the edges of the fabric and sew each of the four corners together. Hem the edges and simply pull the cover over the bench.

PRETTY PLACEMATS

Decorate the table with placemats. We have made some lovely ones from burlap adorned with strips of fabric.

Cut a piece from a burlap sack to your desired placemat size, fraying the edges. Tear a piece of patterned fabric, about ¾" (2 cm) wide. Sew the strip onto the placemat using a sewing machine and fray the edges.

A FABRIC LAMPSHADE

Make something new from something old. A really old and ghastly lampshade from a yard sale can be transformed into something unique with fabric.

The lampshade had a solid frame that was simply wrapped with strips of material from a new piece of fabric. The exposed bulb is an excellent light source.

- Remove all the old fabric from the frame.
- Cut pieces of fabric into strips, around ½" (1.5 cm) wide. It doesn't matter if the fabric frays.
- Cover the whole frame with fabric strips, gluing the fabric at the ends and anywhere necessary. You can swap between colors and fabrics depending on your personal taste.
- Insert a large globe bulb.

FOOTSTOOL RUG

A match made in heaven—an old rug meets a newly purchased footstool. Together they make a lovely piece of movable furniture.

The rug was sewn into a cover for the footstool, and the fringe on the ends give it a fun extra detail. We attached four wheels onto the footstool in lieu of the legs it came with, because this makes it much easier to move.

- Choose a rug that isn't too thick, as it needs to be sewn into the cover. Measure and cut the parts you need for the cover.
- Cut out three pieces of rug: one for the top and the two sides, and two smaller pieces for the other sides/corners. Make sure you add an additional inch (2.5 cm) for the seam allowance.
- Sew the pieces together, right sides together.
- Turn inside out.
- Pull over the footstool.
- Screw on the four wheels.

DRESS

This dress was an improvised project that we hope will inspire you to make something of your own. We don't really have any detailed instructions on how to make it, but we sewed it completely by hand.

To make the skirt, we cut up an old, thin, freshly washed comforter cover with a vibrant color and sewed it together. The completed skirt was then sewn onto a T-shirt. All the seams are sewn right-side up and all the edges have been frayed.

POUF

Another comforter cover found a good home when one of our poufs was in need of reupholstering.

With the new fabric, the pouf became much more pleasing to the eye, while remaining just as comfy to sit on.

- Measure the pouf and add ½" (1.5 cm) for a seam allowance and cut out the pieces from the fabric.
- Cut two round pieces for the top and bottom, as well as a piece for the edge.
- Sew the edge and one of the round pieces together, with right sides together, using a straight stitch and then a zigzag stitch.
- Sew the other round piece in the same way but leave a gap for stuffing.
- Stuff the pouf inside and then sew the gap shut from the outside.

PRINTED CUSHION

An exceptionally fun modern handicraft is decorating neutral-colored linen with fabric paint, woven ribbons, and tassels.

The pattern was made using an Indian-patterned stamp. These can be found in craft stores.

- Iron out any creases in the fabric.
- Dip the stamp in the fabric paint.
- Print the pattern.
- Dry.
- Fix the pattern by ironing over it. Follow the instructions on the paint packaging.
- Sew it onto a cushion cover.
- Sew on a ribbon for decoration.
- Attach a tassel in each corner.

HOW TO MAKE A TASSEL:

- Wind some yarn over four fingers—the more yarn you use the fluffier the tassel will be.
- Pull the yarn off your fingers and tie in the middle with a new piece of yarn.
- Cut the yarn at both ends.
- Tousle the ends. You may need to trim them to make them even.

CHRISTMAS BUNTING

A cozy Christmas with mulled wine, crafts, an open fire, and a ceiling decorated with bunting.

Indoor bunting at Christmas is a unique and quaint way to decorate. It is also super easy to make your own; the bunting is simply triangles sewn onto some ribbon. We used some secondhand, red and white kitchen towels for our flags.

- Measure and draw a triangle on a piece of cardboard in the desired size.
- Cut out the template.
- Place the template on the towel and cut the desired number of flags out using a pair of pinking shears.
- Pin the flags onto a piece of ribbon and sew them on.

WOOD

We do a lot of woodworking and we're quite fond of paneling. We will often dress something in wood and we always finish off with white paint. Walls, wardrobes, and kitchen shelves are a few examples of things we like to make from wood, but we also enjoy making storage boxes. Old windows are another favorite that belong in this chapter. Windows are a source of inspiration for us and can be made into anything from a gardening bench to a picture frame.

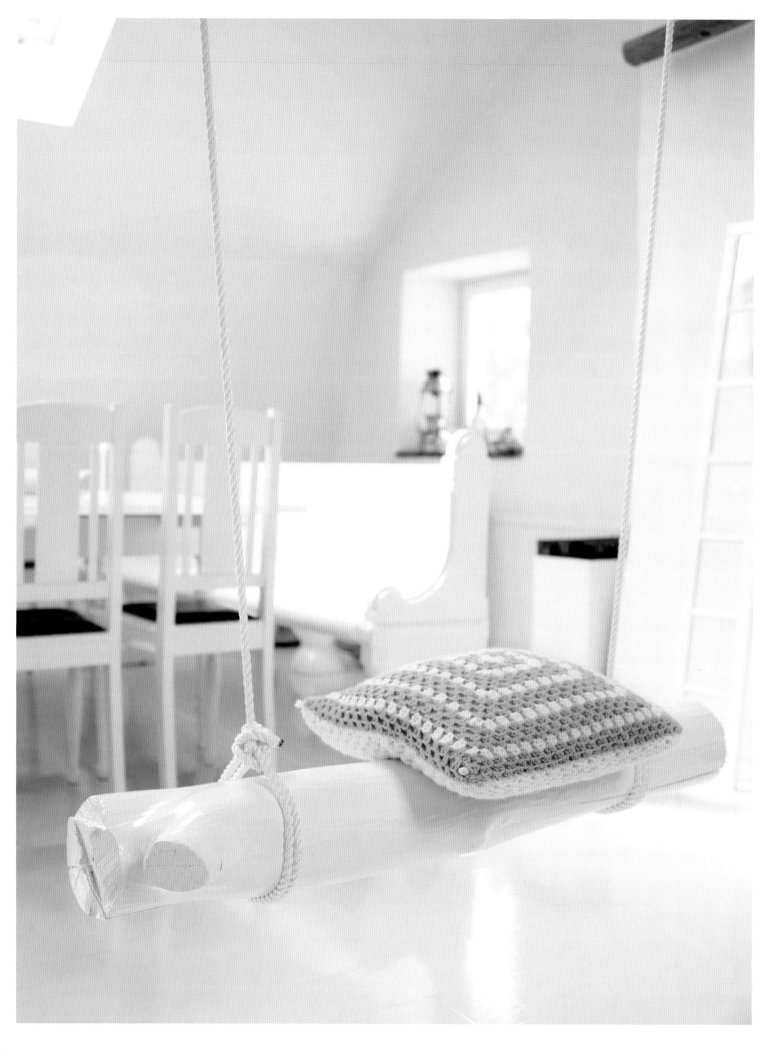

WHITE WOODEN SWING

This swing made from a piece of wood makes a great addition to this living room, and yes, you really can swing on it.

The wood was painted a glossy white and mounted on thick rope of the same color.

- Cut a piece of strong tree trunk to the desired size.
- Remove the bark.
- Clean and sand the wood as best as you can.
- Paint with a primer for woodwork and furniture.
- Finish off with a top coat for woodwork and furniture.
- Let dry.
- Measure and cut two pieces of strong white rope.
- Tie the rope around the wood and hang it up.

A NATURAL LADDER

This charming ladder is made from fallen tree branches and a bit of white paint. It looks lovely leaned against a wall and can be used to hang towels.

   The material for this ladder was found in the woods. We started off by removing any loose bark and moss and then left it to dry. Then, we painted it with wood paint.

- Go out into the woods and look for fallen branches that are the right size.
- Remove loose bark, dirt, and moss and make sure the wood is dry.
- Saw two pieces of slightly thicker branches as straight as possible, around 80" (2 m) in length.
- Saw four pieces to make the rungs, around 16" (40 cm) wide.
- Screw or nail the rungs into the long branches.
- Paint with a primer for woodwork and furniture.
- Finish off with a top coat for woodwork and furniture.

COUNTRY KITCHEN

Many people dream about a real old-fashioned country kitchen where they can cook and socialize. We made this dream come true using pretty simple methods.

The interior was made using IKEA base cabinets and the most standard doors. We then dressed the cupboard doors with paneling that we painted white. The floor paneling runs parallel to the paneling on the cupboards, giving it an old-fashioned feel. The original walls were already paneled, which we discovered when we pulled down the smooth, modern wall. The paneling was cleaned and painted white, with the exception of one wall, which we left worn, to give the room that additional charm. A porcelain sink enhances the rustic look, as do the handles and knobs, which all have an old-fashioned appearance.

The open shelves also add to the country style while making it easy to reach glasses, plates, and other things that are frequently used.

You can get loose pieces of shelving in hardware stores, and you can also

find brackets in various sizes and styles. To make the shelf look more "used" and to enhance the country-style feel, you can saw a bit off the edge or corner of the shelf, and finish off by routing the whole edge. Finally, you can paint the shelving and brackets using a base and top coat in a color of your choice.

Using a wood router, you can give a lovely finish to anything from wooden surfaces to windowsills. The kitchen surfaces were given soft corners as an additional touch. The sharp corner was sawn off, the edge routed, and then the corner was sanded down for a soft finish. Finally the whole bench was treated with oil.

TIPS FOR A COUNTRY KITCHEN:

- Dress the walls and cupboard doors with white paneling.
- Forget using doors on the upper cupboards and place open shelves on brackets.
- Routed edges on shelves and surfaces give a more "used" impression.
- Wooden floors look great sanded down and treated with white oil.
- Let the floor paneling run parallel with the bottom cupboards to give an old-fashioned feel.
- Details like wall sockets, handles, and knobs can do a lot for the overall effect.
- Decorate with old items that are personal to you.
- Old rag rugs create a country feel.

A BRANCH HOOK

Nature is filled with nifty hooks in a variety of shapes and sizes. Here we have a lovely hook that is perfect for shawls and scarves. This hook made from a branch hangs very nicely on the wall.

- Find a branch that fits your needs.
- Saw it down to the right size.
- Measure and mark a spot where you want to place the hook.
- Drill two holes in the branch, one at the top and one at the bottom.
- Attach the branch with two screws.

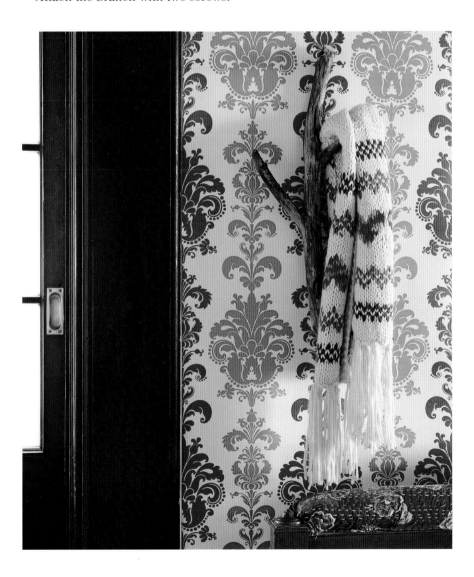

A DIFFERENT KIND OF WALL LAMP

Create a wall lamp from a bracket, a large globe lightbulb and a colorful chord!

It looks great in the hallway and it is made quite simply from a standard wooden bracket, which you can find in a hardware store or at IKEA. These days, most stores selling lamps also sell power chords covered in fabric and big globe lightbulbs. To fit the power chord, widen the existing holes using a drill and make a new hole at the bottom.

- Thread the power chord through the holes of the bracket (refer to the photographs).
- Screw the lightbulb into the chord.
- Screw the bracket onto the wall.

SUPER STORAGE

This is a practical and versatile piece of furniture that works well in our cottage. A box with wheels can be used to store newspapers and plastic bottles that are waiting to be recycled, and when necessary, it can be an excellent place to sit. The wheels make it portable and very versatile.

The box is built from planks that have not been planed and are put together using triangular molding. Hinges are affixed under the lid, and the wheels make it easy to move. Why not make several and put them next to each other. See also page 46.

YOU WILL NEED:

- Lumber, planks (that have not been planed). This box is 30" (74 cm) wide, 17" (44 cm) high, and 16" (40 cm) deep. You can make your box any size you see fit.
- Triangular molding
- Regular molding or lath (for the lid)
- Primer for woodwork
- Paint for woodwork
- Wheels
- A hinge

- Measure and saw the planks and molding to the desired size. The box consists of two short sides, two long sides, a lid, and a bottom piece.
- Start by making the two short ends. Place three planks together. Attach two pieces of triangular molding with two screws in each from the outside.
- Continue with the long sides by screwing on the three side pieces one by one onto both of the end pieces.
- You should now have a rectangular box without a base or lid. Attach the bottom planks using screws; it doesn't matter if there are a few gaps between them.
- The lid is made in the same fashion as the ends. Place three pieces of wood together and attach them using two pieces of molding.
- Using screws, attach the hinge on the box and lid.
- Paint with primer and then a top coat.
- Attach the four wheels with screws.

1. Start with the two short sides. Place three pieces of wood together and screw two pieces of triangular molding on from the outside, with two screws in each one. **2.** Continue with the long sides by screwing the three pieces of wood onto the ends, one by one. **3.** The four sides of the box are held together by the triangular molding in the corners. **4.** For the bottom piece, use two planks, it doesn't matter if there is a small gap between them. The pieces are screwed on to the sides. **5.** The lid is constructed in the same way as the sides. Place three pieces together and attach by screwing them onto two pieces of molding. Add the four wheels, which should have a breaking mechanism, using screws.

SEATING YOUR GUESTS

Finally we can use our pretty wooden spools. By carefully making a slit in them using a saw, they become the perfect place card holders and can be used when setting the table.

The decoration on the card was made with a decorative stitch on a sewing machine.

- Hunt for old wooden spools at thrift stores.
- Using a thin saw, make a slit in the top.
- Cut out a piece of paper.
- Sew on a decorative stitch with a sewing machine.
- Write the guest's name on the card.
- Place in the slit.

DIPPING

We've started dipping objects and furniture in paint. It's lots of fun and the results look great! These wooden salad utensils look super cute after we dipped the handles.

- Make sure the wood is clean and dry.
- Dip the handle into the colored paint, which should be an enamel for furniture and wood.
- Hang them up to dry.

KNEE-HIGH SOCKS

This cute table was saved from the scrap heap . . . and with half-painted legs it became a pretty coffee table for our cottage.

When something this long needs to be dipped, it can be easier to put some masking tape on it and use a paintbrush instead.

We made a plaque from a window, old photos, and cutouts.

WONDERFUL WINDOWS

Old mullioned windows are attractive and charming, and they need to be preserved. Keep an eye out at yard sales and auctions or look online for secondhand windows. They come in all shapes and sizes and can be used as more than just a mere window. Here are some ideas.

FRAME IT

A window with four windowpanes is perfect to use as a frame. We made a plaque using old photos and cutouts.

For the background we used some pretty wrapping paper.

- Measure and cut the wrapping paper.
- Glue the pictures and cutouts onto the window panes in the correct position.
- Measure and saw a piece of Masonite to use as backing.
- Place the wrapping paper in the correct position and nail the Masonite onto the window frame using small nails.

You need planks and a window to make a greenhouse box.

The box is made from two frames placed on top of each other and screwed together using pieces of wood in the four corners.

GROWING

A secondhand window is great to use if you want to build a greenhouse box. We made a simple version and grew some lettuce and herbs in it.

It looks adorable and our plants are growing healthily. Before we planted anything, we treated the wood with oil, painted it with primer, and then painted a top coat using outdoor paint to make it durable. The box consists of two frames on top of each other, which are held together with pieces of wood in the four corners.

When the box needs to be shut, the window is lowered onto the rim and when it needs to stay open, it can be propped up using a piece of wood.

- Measure the length and width of the window you plan to use and saw eight plank pieces: four the window's width and four the window's length.
- The two frames are screwed together and placed on top of each other and held together with pieces of wood that are screwed onto the four corners.
- Treat with oil, use a primer, and then paint a top coat for outside use.
- Attach the window using two hinges.
- Dig out some of the earth where you plan to place your greenhouse box.
- Place the box in its spot and fill it with soil.

Make as many shelves as there are mullions.

A TEENY DISPLAY CASE

Here's a cozy living room with a lovely homemade display case on the wall. We used a nice window for the door and lined the inside with fabric to hide any mess.

- Measure the window as the height and width of the cupboard will be adapted to fit the window.
- There should be a shelf at each mullion, so make as many shelves as there are mullions, as well as a top and bottom shelf.
- Measure the width of the window and subtract the thickness of the side frame.
- Make the shelves from planks or MDF (medium-density fiberboard).
- Make the sides of the cabinet as high as the window. We used paneling for the sides. Drill holes, glue, and then use screws to attach the shelves to the ends.
- Make the back piece from something like Masonite and saw to the right size. It should have the same dimensions as the frame you are using for the door.
- Attach the back piece to the frame using nails.
- Attach the window with two hinges on one side of the cabinet.
- Paint with a primer and top coat in the color of your choice using wood paint.
- Screw on a latch so you can close the door.

A KITCHEN CABINET

We made a large cabinet for our kitchen from these two beautiful windows. We chose the spot for it in the kitchen first, and then made the cabinet according to these measurements.

The walls were made using slats that were covered with paneling on the inside and outside. Everything was painted white. The two windows were attached using hinges. The doors look great—slightly worn and scuffed, but this just enhances the overall effect. The inside was furnished with sturdy shelves placed on ledges.

WHERE TO FIND OLD WINDOWS:

– Auctions
– Family and friends who are throwing theirs out
– Certain antique shops
– Recycling centers selling goods
– Thrift stores around the country

We are recycling this pallet. To avoid big gaps, we filled the spaces with a molding-like material or a piece of lath. The pallet is first painted with a primer and then with a top coat that is suitable for furniture.

Using a template, a sponge, and some paint, we created a pretty pattern and dabbed it on with craft paint.

RECYCLE A PALLET

Use an old pallet to create an unusual table. First you need to fill the gaps between the slats. Then paint and decorate using templates, and you'll end up with a unique, one of a kind table. When the tabletop is finished you can add four large wheels, which make the table movable and versatile. Just like that, an old pallet gets revitalized!

- Clean the pallet if necessary.
- Saw some molding or lath to the right size so they fit the gaps/cracks in the panels.
- Attach them to the gaps using nails.
- Paint with primer.
- Paint a top coat.
- Make a pattern using a template and craft paint.
- Screw four wheels onto it.

A KOOKY CALENDAR

Here we've made a new type of advent calendar with the help of Mother Nature and a few scraps of fabric. We chose to make an "every other day" calendar, which means 12 days of gift giving.

The calendar makes a great addition to the rest of the Christmas decorations. Here are some ideas of what you can place inside the rolls.

- Jewelry
- Gift certificates
- Scratch cards
- Money
- A message—I love you!

- Find a branch in the woods, preferably an old and dry one.
- Measure and saw into the height you desire, ours is around 2' (70 cm).
- Measure and mark out where you want to drill the holes and then drill the desired number into the branch. These holes should be 1" (2.5 cm) in diameter.
- Remove the bark and the branch is ready to use.
- Cut pieces of fabric in different sizes and cut some fringes on both sides. Our fabric pieces all measure 8" (20 cm) wide. The longest one is 16" with 4" long fringes on each side (40 cm + 10 cm fringes). The shortest one is 4" with 4" fringes on each side (10 cm + 10 cm fringes).
- Cut out pieces of paper that have the same dimensions as the pieces of fabric. Using the pieces of paper, wrap the gifts into a roll shape. Wrap the fabric around the roll.
- Tie the ends with yarn or string and place the rolls in the holes in the branch. The longest ones should be at the bottom and the shortest at the top.

YARN

Handicrafts and yarn go hand in hand, and really, we love yarn. Crocheting is probably our favorite hobby, but there is so much more that can be done with yarn. A basket filled with colorful balls of yarn is a simple and lovely way to decorate. Crocheting a necklace is a great starter project that can be followed up with bunting made from granny squares. We also love the crocheted African flower, which is very fun to make—just try it and see!

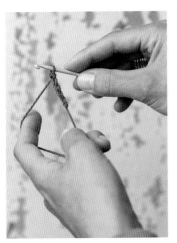   

AFRICAN FLOWER

Learn to crochet an African flower and you'll never stop. . . . The color combinations are endless so you won't get bored, and there is so much you can do with these flowers. Crochet one or crochet several and be inspired by our ideas.

    We used Soft Cotton yarn with a 4/E (3.5 mm) crochet hook.

- Make five chain stitches.
- Make a closed circle using a slip stitch in the first chain stitch.
- Crochet in the ring of chain stitches: 2 double crochets and 1 chain stitch, 6 times.
- Change color. Crochet in every chain stitch: 2 double crochets, 1 chain stitch, 2 double crochets, 6 times.
- Crochet 7 double crochets in every chain stitch.
- Change color. Crochet 1 single crochet in every double crochet, and between every flower petal make 1 double crochet—do this by going in between the two groups of 2 double crochets.
- Change color. Crochet 1 double crochet every single crochet except in the center of the petal, where you do 1 double crochet, 1 chain stitch, 1 double crochet in the same single crochet, creating the corners of the hexagon.
- Secure the yarn and snip off any thread. Voilà! A finished flower!

CARRY YOUR CROCHET WORK

Any type of bag can be decorated with an African flower. Here we have a straw bag that has been adorned with a flower on each side. The bag is great for running errands but can also be used at home to store newspapers.

FLOWERS FOR YOUR FLOWERS

Here is a regular white flowerpot that has been given a border of crocheted flowers. Make about five flowers. Measure your pot to make sure that they fit. Sew them together with overcast stitching and pull over the pot.

AFRICAN FLOWER CUSHION

In a country cottage crocheted cushions look really beautiful. We made 55 flowers and sewed them together to make one piece that was then sewn into a cushion cover.

Each flower has its own unique color combination, but they were all finished off with white yarn to tie the colors together. You will have to custom sew the cover to fit the cushion. The flowers may have to overlap slightly to fit.

SUPER SUMMER THROW

A great project that takes quite some time to make. All the flowers have different color combinations, which varies the work. This throw is made from 64 crocheted flowers that were all finished off with a beige color on the last round. Put all the flowers together and sew together using overcast stitching.

ONE IS ENOUGH

If you just want to make one flower, you can use it to decorate something such as a cushion. Here, we matched the flower with a crocheted granny square blanket. Make one flower and sew it using overcast stitching onto a single-colored pillowcase.

NECKLACE

The crocheted necklace is a great accessory that everyone will admire. It is a fun project that makes an excellent present. The materials do not take up a lot of room so it's great to take with you when traveling.

The necklace is made from Soft Cotton yarn and a 4/E (3.5 mm) hook.

MAKE 20 ROUNDS IN YOUR CHOICE OF COLOR AS FOLLOWS:

- Make 5 chain stitches, make a closed circle with 1 slip stitch in the first chain stitch.
- Round1: Make 8 single crochets by going into the circle.
- Round 2: Make 2 single crochets in every single crochet. Finish off by securing with 1 slip stitch.

CROCHET THE ROUNDS TOGETHER TO MAKE A NECKLACE:

Change color. Crochet a single crochet around half of one circle (8 stitches), and increase with one stitch in every second stitch. Continue with 10 chain stitches. Then crochet a single stitch around half of the next circle in the same way and continue with another 10 chain stitches. Repeat until all the circles are attached. Close the necklace using one slip stitch and secure any loose ends.

EMBROIDERING METAL

We got the idea for this when we found these pots at IKEA. As suspected it's perfect for embroidering!

Choose pretty embroidery floss and sew through the holes, making the pot unique and personal.

A CROCHETED BORDER

Here's a cozy table setting decorated in soft colors with yarn and lace. The placemats from IKEA were given brand new borders made of pink yarn—a simple way to make them stand out.

The edge was crocheted using Molly yarn and an 8/H (5 mm) hook with two rounds of single crochets around the placemat.

A LONG-TERM PROJECT

Not all projects have to be finished right away. Sometimes it's nice to have a piece of work that takes time to complete, looks great lying around, and can be picked up whenever you have a spare minute. The next piece is the beginning of a crocheted bedspread that will take forever to finish.

The bedspread can be left out and worked on every now and then. Colors and types of stitching can be improvised and switched up as you move along.

- Measure the bed and crochet as many chain stitches as desired.
- Round 1: Crochet 1 single crochet in the second chain stitch from the hook and then continue with single crochets to the end of the row.
- Round 2: Crochet 1 chain stitch and then continue with single crochets to the end of the row.
- Continue with the rest of the rows using 1 chain stitch and then whatever stitches you want to use. Ours is a mixture of single crochets, double crochets, and half double crochets. Change the color according to your personal preference.
- Crochet until the bedspread is the desired size.

MOBILE

We bought the frame for the mobile and crocheted them into colorful balls, which can be hung for decoration. It takes six granny squares to make a ball. We used Soft Cotton yarn and a 4/E (3.5 mm) hook.

- Make six small granny squares with three rows in each one. Finish each square with yarn in the same color.
- Sew the squares together with overcast stitching. Remember that it needs to be in the shape of a cube/ball.
- When the last square is sewn on, leave a small opening to fill the ball with padding.
- Sew the opening shut.
- Attach a piece of yarn to the ball and hang onto the frame.
- Make five more balls in the same fashion.

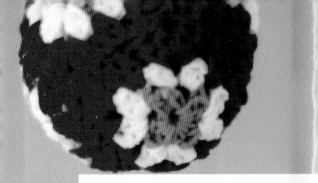

HOW TO MAKE A GRANNY SQUARE:

– Crotchet 5 chain stitches.

– Make a closed ring with a slip stitch in the first chain stitch.

– Make 2 half double crochets by going into the ring, crochet 2 chain stitches, 2 half double crochets by going into the ring. Repeat two more times. Secure with a slip stitch. You should now have a square of chain stitches that makes a corner.

– Switch to another color.

– Make 2 half double stitches in one corner, crochet 2 chain stitches and 2 half double crochets in the same corner. Make 1 chain stitch to get to the next corner.

– Continue in this fashion for the next 2 corners and finish off with 1 chain stitch. Secure with 1 slip stitch and cut the yarn.

– Switch colors and make the next row in the same fashion. Crochet 2 half double crochets in one corner, 2 chain stitches and 2 half double crochets in the same corner. Make 1 chain stitch and then crochet 2 half double crochets in the next hole, make 1 chain stitch. You should now be in the next corner. Make 2 half double crochets, 2 chain stitches, and 2 half double crochets.

– Continue to the end of the row and finish off with 1 chain stitch and then secure with 1 slip stitch.

– If you want a larger square, continue with more rows in the same way.

For pictures and further instruction on how to make a granny square, check out our other books or visit our blog:
www.sannaochsania.blogspot.se.

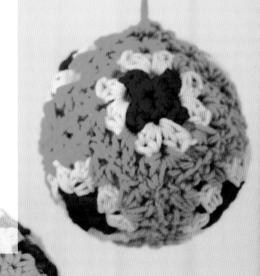

BUNTING

We love bunting because it looks great when it's made from paper and when it's made from fabric. Here is our own favorite version: the crocheted one.

Bunting looks great wherever it's hung up; it's colorful and pretty. Our bunting is made from crocheted granny squares, but instead of rectangular squares, we've made triangular ones. Basically you are making three corners instead of four. The flags are crocheted together using two single crochets.

HOW TO MAKE THE FLAGS:

- Crochet five chain stitches.
- Close to make a ring using 1 slip stitch in the first chain stitch.
- Crochet 2 half double crochets by going into the ring, make 2 chain stitches, then 2 half double crochets by going into the ring. Crochet 2 chain stitches and then repeat the process once more. Secure the chain stitch with a slip stitch and cut the yarn. You should now have a triangle with a chain stitch creating the corner.
- Change yarn to a different color.
- Crochet 2 half double crochets in one corner, crochet 2 chain stitches, then 2 half double crochets in the same corner.
- To get to the next corner, make 1 chain stitch.
- Crochet 2 half double stitches, 2 chain stitches, 2 half double stitches, and then 1 chain stitch to get to the next corner. Continue in this way to the last corner and finish off with 1 chain stitch. Secure with 1 slip stitch and cut the yarn.
- Change to a different colored yarn. Make the next round in the same way. Make 2 half double crochets in one corner, 2 chain stitches, then 2 half double crochets in the same corner. Crochet 1 chain stitch and then 2 half double crochets in the next corner, crochet 1 chain stitch. You should now be in the next corner. Make 2 half double crochets, 2 chain stitches, and 2 half double crochets.
- Continue to the end of the row and finish off with 1 chain stitch and secure with a slip stitch.
- If you want a larger square/flag, you can continue with more rounds in the same fashion. We made these flags using 7 rounds.
- Attach the flags by crocheting 3 rounds using single crochets along one of the sides on all the flags.

Double up the yarn and alternate between wrapping every other strand in front and behind the pins.

USING YARN

A few thoughts on handicrafts . . .

Handicraft, making things by hand, embroidering, and crocheting details, can create a unique environment. Bright colors and materials such as yarn and textiles mean that handicrafts inspire creativity. The handmade items are the focus. In our cupboard we keep all sorts of things that are needed to create a variety of crafts.

We wrapped the back of this thrift store sofa made from rattan using a Lovikka yarn.

YARN AT CHRISTMAS

What can be more charming than a Christmas wreath made from yarn? Hard to beat isn't it?

Pretty, round balls of Christmas-colored yarn are arranged on an old wire hanger. Isn't the result adorable?

- Wind up the desired number of yarn balls, preferably in two different sizes. Make sure they are perfectly round.
- Take a wire hanger and bend it into a circle.
- Cut off the hook using wire cutters.
- Thread the yarn onto the hanger.
- Bend the edges using pliers to make two loops that can hook onto each other. The yarn should be evenly spaced on the hanger. Now, it's ready to be hung up.

PAPER

Paper is an inspiring material and is easy to work with. Cutting and pasting is something everyone starts with at a young age but there's a lot you can do with paper to create unique interior designs. We use wallpaper, wrapping paper, and silk paper. One favorite is authentic vintage wallpaper. It is slightly more fragile to work with, but the patterns and colors are fantastic. Even if you have only a small piece, it will still be enough to dress the hangers in the hallway closet, which is guaranteed to be eye-catching.

HAPPY HANGERS

Old vintage wallpaper is something we adore. If you're lucky you can find some at a thrift store, but you can also purchase it online. If you are dressing hangers, all you need is a small piece.

White hangers from IKEA look great dressed with wallpaper.

- Trace the contours of the hanger on the back of the wallpaper.
- Cut out the shape.
- Glue the wallpaper onto the hanger using spray adhesive or wallpaper paste.
- When the surface has dried it needs to be varnished to make it last. We usually use a floor varnish.

PAPER UPHOLSTERY

Match the vase with the walls and reuse old cans—two simple ideas for what to do with an old scrap of paper or wallpaper.

We dressed a cylindrical glass vase with a pretty piece of floral wallpaper.

Old tin cans were decorated with paper, which we think is a better option than putting them in the recycling bin!

- Make sure the items to be covered are clean and dry.
- Measure and cut the paper.
- Secure the paper with spray adhesive. You can also use double-sided tape if you want to be able to remove the paper.

FLORAL TRAY

More wallpaper! This cute coffee tray was made flowery with the help of some wallpaper—pink roses on a blue background—and lace.

- Make sure the tray is clean and dry.
- Measure and cut the wallpaper to fit the tray.
- Glue the wallpaper using a regular wallpaper paste or spray adhesive. Brush or press out the air bubbles.
- When the glue is dry you should varnish the surface to make it durable. We usually use floor varnish.
- You can glue a pretty lace ribbon around the edge as an extra decoration.

VINTAGE STAR

Here we've used remnants of vintage wallpaper. The star is made by folding 12 square pieces of paper. A tip is to start by folding a star using origami paper about 6" x 6" (15 cm x 15 cm). When you know how to fold it you can always increase the size.

The star looks lovely hanging up and can even be used as an advent star at Christmastime if you choose a slightly more Christmassy paper.

- Fold a square piece of paper down the middle. You should now have a rectangle. Fold the piece of paper down the middle again to make a smaller square. Open the paper back up. You now have a cross that works as guidelines.
- Fold all four corners into the middle.
- Hold the square with one of the corners facing you. Fold one side toward the middle so the edges are in line with the center of the square.
- Do the same on the other side. You should now have a pointed shape that somewhat resembles a diamond.
- Turn it over so the backside is facing up, fold over the point of the diamond that looks shorter and wider. It should now be a triangle.
- Fold the triangle in half along the crease you created earlier. Repeat the steps above until you have the 12 pieces you need to make a star.
- Put the pieces together by sticking them into each other, if you wish you can secure them with a bit of glue.

MATCHING

Spending some extra time on the table settings can really enhance your guests' experience. Here is a decorative napkin ring that is quick to make, using regular wrapping paper. Make a placemat to match the napkin ring. Feel free to use pinking shears.

- Cut a strip of paper with pinking shears and wrap it around a rolled-up napkin. Secure the end with a bit of glue.
- Cut a piece of paper or use a whole sheet in the same pattern, to use as a placemat.

STORAGE

Attractive storage space is something we like to write about so of course we're repeating some ideas in this book. White cardboard boxes from IKEA, shoe boxes, or moving boxes all look fantastic when covered in wallpaper. Mix and match and leave them out to be admired. In this case, we dressed just the sides and left the lids white.

- Measure and cut the wallpaper according to the box's size.
- Use spray adhesive to attach it.

WALLPAPER COLLAGE

(see next page)

The wall above the bed was made into a colorful wallpaper collage. All the wallpaper is from the '70s and looks superb. The wall just above the bed instantly pops with some vibrant wallpaper.

- Measure and cut the wallpaper.
- Plan out ahead of time where you want to place it.
- Use wallpaper glue to place it on the wall.

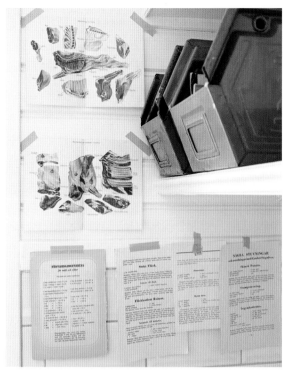

BOOK PAGES

Here's a cozy kitchen with an old-fashioned feel. Open shelves instead of closed cupboards, paneling, and white floorboards help to create that country style. It's a great place to decorate with pages from old books.

Old books can be found cheaply at thrift stores; try to find books with attractive pages and textures.

We found a really old cookbook and put some of the pages up using washi tape, which can be removed without leaving any marks.

DOILIES

This is a classic paper craft that can be spruced up by using doilies. Fold, cut, then unfold. It is fun to make random cuts and just see how it turns out!

- Fold the doily three times in the middle.
- Cut away tabs in any shape you like.
- Unfold to see the result.

POM-POMS

A pom-pom is a fluffy, decorative ball or tassel and is usually very colorful. The material can be wool, cotton, or paper so it's easy to make your own.

Fun pom-poms made of paper are easy to create and look beautiful as party decorations, or to hang over the dinner table or in a window. Feel free to make several in different sizes and colors.

- Layer about 10 pieces of silk paper on top of each other. Cut a square in your desired size.
- Fold the sheets like you would a paper fan.
- Cut the edges to round them.
- Do the same with the edges on the other side.
- Tie together in the middle using a piece of string and pull it slightly.
- Open on one side, sheet by sheet, like a fan. Do the same on the other side.

CHRISTMAS GARLAND

A cute, old-fashioned, and homemade garland looks great on the Christmas tree. Use any paper you like. It can be wrapping paper or wallpaper. All the hearts are sewn into a garland using a sewing machine.

- Fold the paper in half and glue the two halves together so that both sides of the garland are patterned.
- Use a cookie cutter as a template to draw hearts on the paper. Cut them out.
- Use a sewing machine to sew all the hearts together and make a garland.

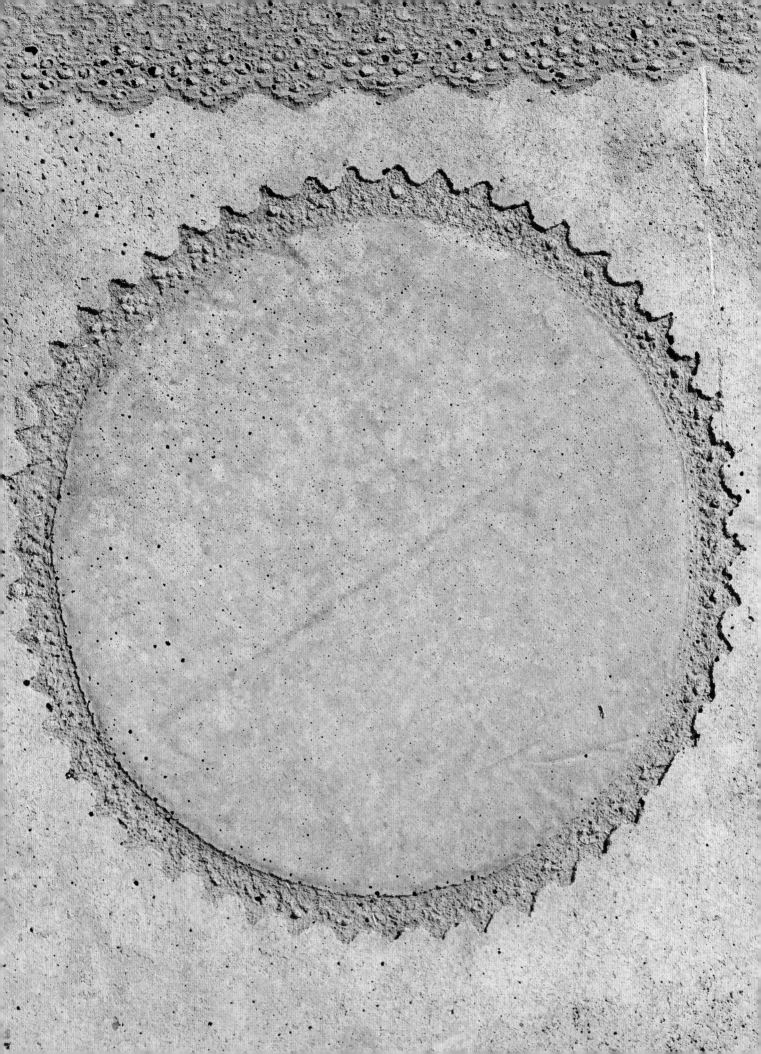

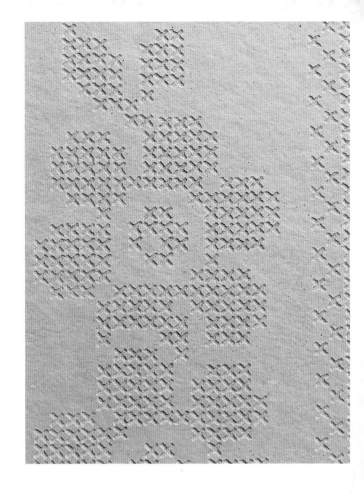

CONCRETE

Concrete is a great material and we've worked a lot with it over the years, so we just had to include it in the book. Concrete is versatile, hardy, and can be used both inside and out. The sizes of these projects vary from very small to enormous. The smaller ones can be made indoors, but if you're casting a larger project, you should really do it outside. As it is quite a cheap material, it is worth experimenting with—something we've done many times with varying results. We always learn by experimenting! One example is when we tried casting concrete eggs in regular eggshells, which worked surprisingly well. The eggs ended up as Easter decorations on our table.

WHAT IS CONCRETE?

Concrete consists of eighty percent aggregate—made up of sand, rock, and gravel—fourteen percent cement, which consists of ground limestone that has been heated up, and six percent water. This basically makes concrete a natural material that is environmentally friendly, useful, and durable. The fine concrete we use is usually quite smooth, as it contains small stones that are a maximum of 4 mm in size. You can find this type of concrete at local hardware stores.

MOLDS

The mold you use to cast concrete in is important, as this is what gives you the finished product. Plastic is great, as it has a smooth surface and easily releases the concrete, but other materials such as strong cardboard, wood, or rubber also work well. It's great if the mold is slightly elastic, too. Brush the inside with some cooking oil and the concrete will release more easily. Buckets and old packaging are examples of good, inexpensive molds. Sometimes you may have to cut the mold to release the concrete. You can also use pretty leaves from nature or textured wallpaper to make patterns in the concrete. Keep your eyes peeled for interesting shapes at secondhand stores. For bigger projects such as tables or work surfaces, you will need to build the mold from particle board and wooden joists. An alternative to particle board is formwork, smooth water-resistant boards that are made especially for casting in concrete. They are a bit more expensive but can be worth it if you plan to make more advanced projects. The concrete doesn't get stuck in the formwork so it can be used again and again. The benefit of building your own mold is that you can customize the dimensions.

REINFORCEMENT

You need to reinforce the concrete when casting larger items. A tabletop, for example, needs to be reinforced so it doesn't break. Reinforcing also makes

the concrete more durable in freezing temperatures. Plus, it's not as complicated as it sounds. To do this, you can use reinforcing bars (rebar), reinforcement mesh, chicken wire, or hardware cloth. The last two options are soft and can be cut with chicken wire. If you use rebar, it needs to be cut at the hardware store where they have the right tools to do so. Ask the staff about reinforcing larger projects to get the right dimensions.

When you reinforce something, you cut a piece of the reinforcement in a size to fit the mold. Press the reinforcement into the wet concrete and, if necessary, add some more concrete to keep it in place. It is important that the reinforcement sits in the center of the concrete.

DRYING TIME

To cure concrete means to let it dry, harden, and gain strength. The length of time it takes depends on the thickness and size of the item cast, but you need to allow at least 24 hours, possibly 48. It is vital that the concrete is left to cure on a flat surface so that is sets evenly. Tabletops are a good example of things that really need to be left to dry flat. It is best to find a spot ahead of time for your concrete to cure. A cool, shaded place is best. If you can, cover the item in plastic—a plastic bag, tarpaulin, or plastic wrap all work. To slow down the curing process it's a good idea to water it by spraying it with water from a spray bottle a few times. Do not remove the item too soon as the likelihood of it breaking is quite high.

MIXING CONCRETE

When you have planned and prepared to cast your item, it's time to mix the concrete. You only need water and fine concrete, which get mixed together. Here is a list of what you need and a description of how to do it. This description applies to all projects.

NOTE! Make sure you have your molds and other items ready before you begin mixing the concrete.

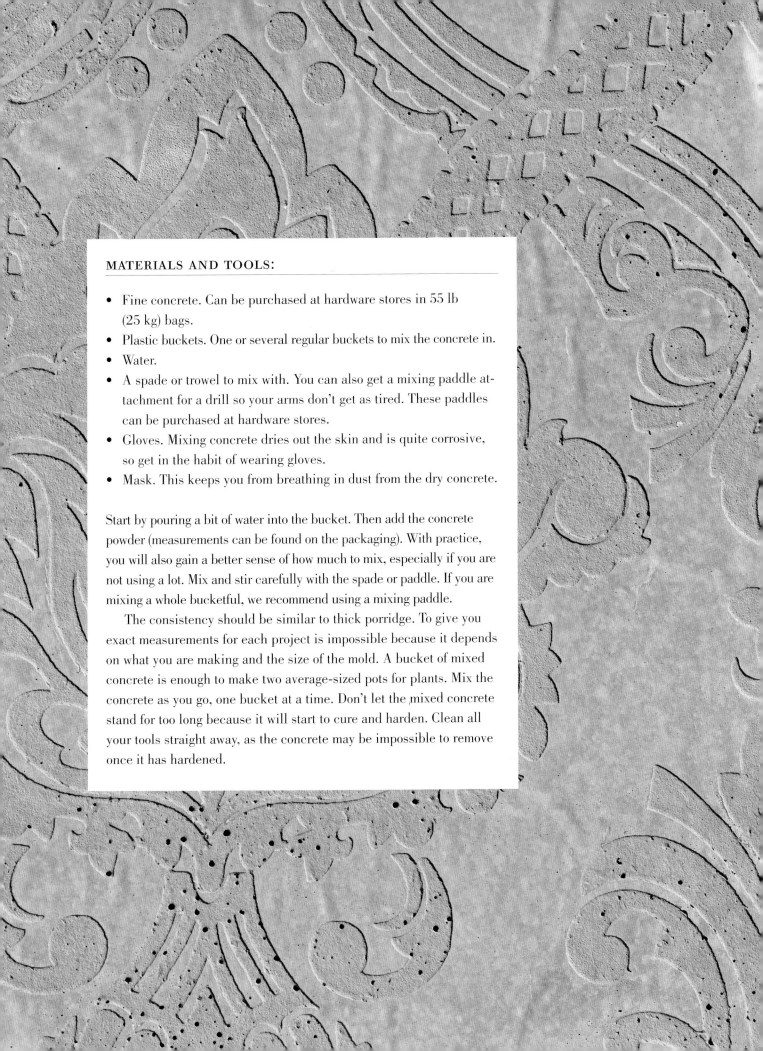

MATERIALS AND TOOLS:

- Fine concrete. Can be purchased at hardware stores in 55 lb (25 kg) bags.
- Plastic buckets. One or several regular buckets to mix the concrete in.
- Water.
- A spade or trowel to mix with. You can also get a mixing paddle attachment for a drill so your arms don't get as tired. These paddles can be purchased at hardware stores.
- Gloves. Mixing concrete dries out the skin and is quite corrosive, so get in the habit of wearing gloves.
- Mask. This keeps you from breathing in dust from the dry concrete.

Start by pouring a bit of water into the bucket. Then add the concrete powder (measurements can be found on the packaging). With practice, you will also gain a better sense of how much to mix, especially if you are not using a lot. Mix and stir carefully with the spade or paddle. If you are mixing a whole bucketful, we recommend using a mixing paddle.

The consistency should be similar to thick porridge. To give you exact measurements for each project is impossible because it depends on what you are making and the size of the mold. A bucket of mixed concrete is enough to make two average-sized pots for plants. Mix the concrete as you go, one bucket at a time. Don't let the mixed concrete stand for too long because it will start to cure and harden. Clean all your tools straight away, as the concrete may be impossible to remove once it has hardened.

CONCRETE AT EASTER

Easter yellow and concrete gray—these colors look beautiful together and make a stunning contrast on the Easter table setting. You can even cast your own concrete Easter eggs in your kitchen—a slightly unusual Easter craft.

We'll start with the small eggs that are made in real egg shells. These make adorable table decorations.

- Mix the concrete according to the instructions on page 103. When you make smaller projects, you can mix the concrete by hand in a bucket.
- Carefully make a hole in each egg with a sharp knife and empty the contents. Carefully rinse the shells.
- Fill the eggshells with concrete using a spoon.
- Place the eggs back in their carton and leave them to cure for 24 hours (no longer as the shells can stick). Tap to remove the shell and you will be left with a pretty concrete egg.

TO MAKE A SLIGHTLY LARGER EGG

- This is made with the help of cardboard Easter eggs. You will need a larger one and a smaller one so you can make concrete bowls to fill with Easter candy.

- If you cast two egg halves, you can put them together to make a whole egg.

- You need a larger and a smaller egg to make the bowl. Mix the concrete according to the instructions on page 103.

- Brush the inside of the larger egg and the outside of the smaller egg with cooking oil as it will loosen more easily.

- Fill the larger egg half with concrete and press the smaller half into the concrete. Don't let it overflow. Carefully tap the egg against the table to remove any air bubbles.

- Place stones or weights in the smaller egg to keep it in place and leave it to cure for 24 hours—make sure it is on a flat surface. Loosen both cardboard eggs from the concrete.

A PRACTICAL STEP

Making a step from a plastic mold is pretty easy and can be a great addition to your outdoor area such as outside a shed, outhouse, or, as we have done, a greenhouse. The pretty Moroccan tiles make a nice addition. It's both attractive and practical for the greenhouse.

- Dig a hole and level the surface where you wish to place the step.
- Measure and saw three boards to make a frame (four if the step is not going against a wall).
- Screw the boards together in the shape you want.
- Place the frame where you want the step to be.
- Fill it with stone or gravel so you won't need as much concrete.
- Mix the concrete according to the instructions on page 103.
- Pour the concrete into the frame or mold.
- Moisten the tiles slightly so they don't absorb too much water from the concrete.
- Carefully press down the tiles.
- Leave the concrete to cure for 48 hours.
- Remove the frame from the concrete step.

CONCRETE POTS

The easiest projects usually turn out the best and that's exactly the case for these pots. We made a few smooth concrete pots using two buckets.

You can see the results here: two classy concrete pots to place around the garden. As the plastic buckets have a shiny surface, the surface of the pots will also be smooth and shiny.

- To make the pot, we used two plastic buckets for our molds. We took a paint bucket and a regular plastic bucket.
- Brush the inside of the paint bucket and the outside of the other bucket with cooking oil. This makes it easier to remove the finished pot from the buckets later.
- Mix the concrete according to the instructions on page 103.
- Pour the concrete into the paint bucket. It should not be completely filled up as there needs to be space to press in the second bucket.
- The regular bucket is pressed into the concrete so the rims of the two buckets line up. Shake the mold by carefully tapping it with a hammer to get rid of any air bubbles.
- Use a few stones as a weight to keep the smaller bucket in place.
- Leave it to cure for at least 24 hours (it should not be left in the sun). For best results, water the concrete a few times while it's drying.
- Remove the weights and loosen the buckets from the pot. If you like, you can cut the outer bucket and leave the bottom in place as this makes the pot waterproof. Sometimes you need to be a bit aggressive and pull, pry, and stretch to get rid of the buckets. If need be, use a pair of pruning shears to cut them off.

This pot is smaller, but is made in exactly the
same way. Just use two smaller buckets.

The pattern from the textured wallpaper is clearly defined in the concrete.

CONCRETE TABLE

With a sheepskin throw and a concrete table, this design is inspired by Gotland, an island off the coast of Sweden. Try to cast a tabletop with a pattern by using some textured wallpaper.

We started off with a small side table from IKEA and used the frame for our concrete table top. To cast a tabletop in concrete you need to make a mold from particle board and joists. The table top is heavy enough to just put in place and "leave" on top. By casting on a piece of textured wallpaper, the surface of the table will have a pattern laid into it. Choose wallpaper with a raised, plastic pattern.

A mixing paddle attached to a drill makes the job easier when it comes to mixing the concrete.

- Measure and screw the joists into the size you desire. Our tabletop measures 21 ¾" × 21 ¾" (55 cm × 55 cm). Screw the joists onto the particle board.
- Cut the wallpaper, which should have a textured, raised pattern.
- Place the wallpaper in the mold with the pattern facing up. The wallpaper should go up over the edges so the tabletop will be patterned all over. This also makes the edges slightly rounded.
- For the surface to be durable it needs to be reinforced. Chicken wire works well and is easy to cut. Cut the chicken wire to fit the mold.
- Mix the concrete according to the instructions on page 103.
- Pour the concrete in the mold on top of the wallpaper. Make a layer approximately 2" (5 cm) thick.
- Gently tap the mold against the ground a few times to get rid of any air bubbles, as this will smooth the surface and enhance the pattern.
- Press the reinforcement into the concrete so it is completely covered.
- Tap the mold against the ground again to get rid of any air bubbles.
- Leave the concrete to cure for at least 24 hours, preferably longer. Make sure that it's standing on a flat surface and out of the sun. For the best results, water the concrete a few times during the drying time using a spray bottle.
- Carefully pry the tabletop from the mold and pull off the wallpaper.

CONCRETE IN THE KITCHEN

A tabletop and a work surface are made the same way. In this kitchen, the original counter space had a standard measurement that was too short. So as a clever solution we made an extra surface from concrete. To decorate, we used some Moroccan tiles, which look fantastic in the concrete. The slightly uneven edge just adds to the charm.

- The shape for the work surface is made from plywood and regular joists that you can buy from the hardware store.
- Measure the size of the work surface and screw the joists together to fit the required size.
- Screw the joists onto the plywood.
- Place double-sided tape (carpet tape) on the front of the tiles so that the tape covers the whole tile but not the edges. This means that they stay in place and don't get covered in concrete.
- Moisten the tiles so that they don't soak up too much water from the concrete.
- Place the tiles where you want them with the back facing up.
- For the surface to be durable it needs to be reinforced with chicken wire cut to size.
- Mix the concrete according to the instructions on page 103.
- Pour the concrete into the mold.
- Shake the mold by gently tapping it with a hammer to remove any air bubbles.
- Press the reinforcement into the concrete so it is completely covered by the concrete (it needs to be in the "center" of the concrete).
- Shake the mold by gently tapping it with a hammer to remove any air bubbles.
- Leave the concrete to cure for at least 24 hours. Make sure it is on a flat surface and not in the sun. For the best results, water the concrete a few times while it dries.
- Carefully loosen the work surface from the mold by gently prying it out, and remove the tape from the tiles.
- Place the work surface where you want it and, if possible, treat it to avoid stains.

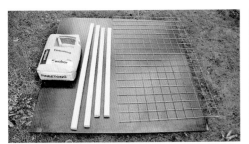  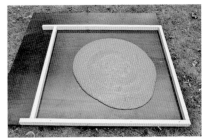

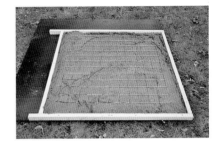

A NEW PATIO TABLE

Spring is here and we're having fun fixing up our patio. We made a table from some stained wood and concrete. Perfect for breakfast!

We made a base frame from joists that we painted with an attractive stain. You can use any frame for the base you like—maybe from a secondhand table or some trestle table legs from IKEA.

The tabletop is made from concrete and once in place, it is ready to use. This tabletop looks better and better as the years go by.

- Make the tabletop frame from plywood and joists purchased from the hardware store.
- Measure the size you want the tabletop to be and screw the joists together to the desired shape.
- Screw the joists onto the plywood.
- To make the top durable it should be reinforced with mesh, which should be cut to size.
- Mix the concrete according to the instructions on page 103.
- Pour the concrete into the frame.
- Press the mesh into the concrete so that it is entirely covered by the concrete. It should be placed in the middle of the concrete.
- Shake the frame by gently tapping it with a hammer to get out any air bubbles.
- Allow the tabletop dry for at least 24 hours and make sure it's lying flat and not in the sun. For best results water the concrete a few times while it's drying.
- Gently pry the frame to loosen it.
- Place the top onto the frame/legs.

MINI LEAVES

This is a version of the popular rhubarb leaf made from concrete. It is made using the same method but with a much smaller leaf.

These mini leafs are very cute to arrange jewelry on, for example, and the veins on the leaf clearly come through in the concrete.

- Pick some clean, attractive leaves outside.
- Make a small mound of sand or soil and place a leaf, bottom side up, on top.
- Mix the concrete according to the instructions on page 103.
- Place the concrete on the leaf.
- Even out the concrete so it covers the leaf. Try to make the edges even.
- Allow the leaf to dry for at least 24 hours in the shade. For the best results, water the concrete once during the drying period by spraying some water on it.
- Carefully remove the leaf from the concrete.

CASTING AT CHRISTMAS

Merry Christmas! For Christmas we made a lovely, numbered advent candleholder from a cake tin. Casting an object from concrete is like making a cake—just with a heavier batter. The candleholder was really pretty with some shards of red and white porcelain mixed in. The candles are lit and we're full of the Christmas spirit. This candleholder has numbers molded into the concrete. Paper numbers can be purchased at hobby or craft stores.

To decorate, we placed small shards of porcelain from a patterned saucer into the wet concrete. You can find a cheap one at a thrift store.

- Use a long Teflon cake tin, numbers made from cardboard, and a small porcelain saucer, preferably with a pattern.
- Wrap the plate in a newspaper or a towel so the shards don't go flying, and crush the plate with a hammer.
- Place the numbers, reversed, on the inside of the cake tin with double-sided tape or a glue gun.
- Brush the inside of the tin with cooking oil.
- Mix the concrete according to the instructions on page 103.
- Pour the concrete into the tin until it's just about at the top.
- Carefully tap the tin against the floor several times to get rid of any air bubbles.
- Push the four candles, around ¾" (2 cm) in size, into the concrete. They will stand securely on their own. (When they have burned all the way down, there is automatically a hole for a new candle!)
- Carefully press the porcelain shards, in the pattern of your choice, into the wet concrete by tapping them gently.
- Leave the candleholder to dry for at least 24 hours on a flat surface.
- Tip the candleholder out of the tin.

Apart from concrete, you will need the following to make an advent candle: a Teflon cake tin, a porcelain coffee saucer, numbers made from heavy-duty cardboard, and four wax candles.

Place the numbers, backward, on the inside of the cake tin with doublesided tape or by using a glue gun.

When the mold is ready, mix up the concrete. You can do this in a plastic bowl with a spatula.

Fill the mold almost to the edge and place the four candles into the concrete. They will stand securely.

Carefully press some porcelain shards in a pattern of your choice, into the wet concrete.